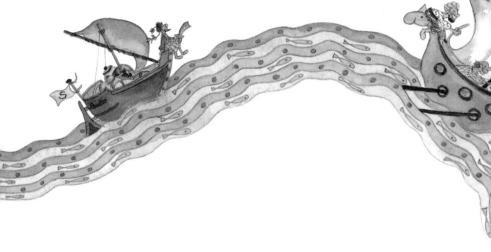

Copyright © 1994 by Marcia Williams

All rights reserved.

First U.S. edition 1994
Published in Great Britain in 1994 by
Walker Books Ltd., London.

Library of Congress Cataloging-in-Publication Data

Williams, Marcia.
Sinbad the sailor / Marcia Williams.—1st U.S. ed.
Summary: Uses a comic strip format to present the
seven voyages of Sinbad, in which he encounters a
colossal giant, a sea monster, and other dangers.
ISBN 1-56402-310-9
1. Sinbad the Sailor (Legendary character)
[1. Fairy tales.   2. Folklore, Arab.   3. Cartoons
and comics.]   I. Sinbad the sailor.   II. Title.
PN6727.W475S56   1994
741.5'973—dc20   93-3531

10 9 8 7 6 5 4 3 2 1

Printed in Italy

The pictures in this book were done in ink
and watercolor.

Candlewick Press
2067 Massachusetts Avenue
Cambridge, Massachusetts 02140

Sinbad the Sailor

Retold and illustrated by
Marcia Williams

CANDLEWICK PRESS
CAMBRIDGE, MASSACHUSETTS

Long ago, in Baghdad, there lived a poor, discontented man named Sinbad the Porter.

One day, weary and cross from carrying his heavy load,

the porter sat down to rest outside a rich merchant's home.

As he sat there, grumbling about the unfairness of life,

the wealthy merchant, who had overheard him, sent out a page. The page took Sinbad the Porter by the hand and led him up the path and into the house.

There, the elderly merchant, Sinbad the Sailor, sat feasting with his noble friends.
The porter was overwhelmed by such grandeur, but he was
made welcome and invited to share the feast.

SINBAD'S FIRST VOYAGE

"We left the port of Basra with our ship well loaded. Through night

and day we sailed, bartering our goods from land to land until, at last,

we reached an island as fair as the Garden of Eden.

Once ashore, I set off to explore, while my friends built a fire.

Suddenly the island started shaking, and the captain yelled:

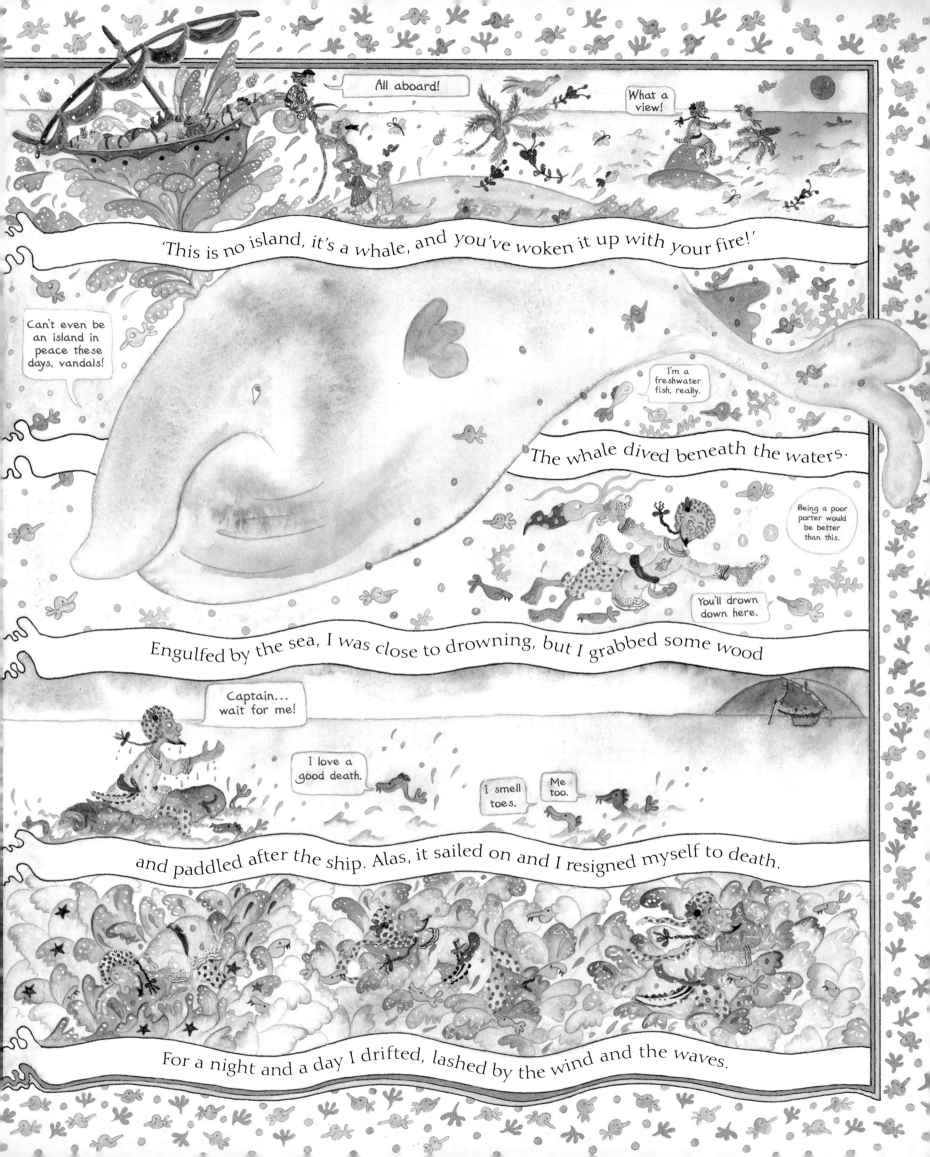

As luck would have it, I was washed ashore onto a wooded island.

I lay exhausted until the morning sun roused me.

My poor feet were swollen from many fish bites,

but, cutting myself a staff, I hobbled off to explore.

I soon came upon a beautiful mare tethered to a tree and

guarded by a well-armed but sleepy groom.

He told me that the mare belonged to King Mahraza.

Just as I was telling him of my great adventure,

the mare started screaming. Turning toward her, we saw a sea horse trying to drag the mare into the ocean. We rushed to save her, and, by yelling and waving with great energy, we managed to drive the sea horse away.

The groom then took me to King Mahraza's beautiful palace.

On hearing how I had helped to save his fine mare,

the delighted king made me Controller of Shipping

and heaped many magnificent treasures upon me.

In spite of his great kindness, I longed to return home.

So you can imagine my delight when, one joyous day,

the ship arrived on which I had originally set sail.

It had the very same captain and all my valuable goods,

from which I chose several fine gifts for the kindly king.

He, in return, gave me yet more sparkling presents

and wished me a safe and trouble-free homeward journey.

After many days' sailing, I arrived once more at Baghdad.

There I bought lavish houses and rich farmland.

I entertained my friends with the best food and wine.

But eventually I began to forget the dangers of my voyage

and long, once more, for the excitement of traveling at sea.

That is the story of my first voyage.
Tomorrow, if Allah wills it, I shall tell you the tale of my second voyage—which,
although you will find it hard to believe, was even more amazing."

SINBAD'S SECOND VOYAGE

"Once again I set sail from Basra with other merchants.

From port to port we bartered our merchandise,

until we reached an uninhabited island, where we landed.

Leaving my companions, I went off to find a shady spot.

Having eaten my lunch, I settled down to sleep.

When I awoke, I realized that I was all alone and that my ship was fast disappearing over the horizon.

Quickly I climbed a tall tree and surveyed the island.

All I could see was a strange white object in the distance.

So I made my way across the island to investigate.

It was a huge white thing, without windows or doors, at least fifty paces around, and too smooth to climb. While I stood puzzling over it, the sky suddenly became as dark as night.

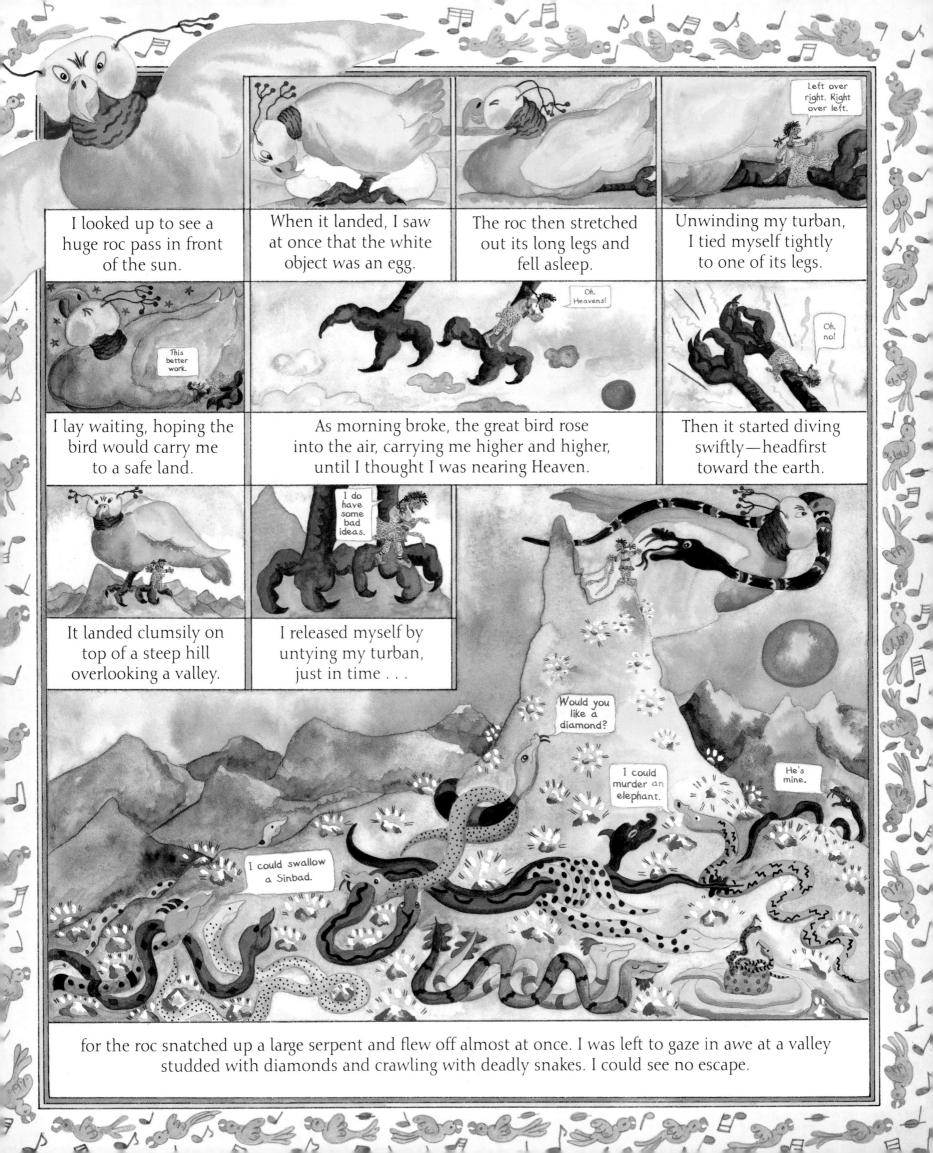

I looked up to see a huge roc pass in front of the sun.

When it landed, I saw at once that the white object was an egg.

The roc then stretched out its long legs and fell asleep.

Unwinding my turban, I tied myself tightly to one of its legs.

I lay waiting, hoping the bird would carry me to a safe land.

As morning broke, the great bird rose into the air, carrying me higher and higher, until I thought I was nearing Heaven.

Then it started diving swiftly—headfirst toward the earth.

It landed clumsily on top of a steep hill overlooking a valley.

I released myself by untying my turban, just in time . . .

for the roc snatched up a large serpent and flew off almost at once. I was left to gaze in awe at a valley studded with diamonds and crawling with deadly snakes. I could see no escape.

Luckily I found a cave to rest in that night,

although even there I was not entirely safe.

The next morning, as I emerged into the sunlight,

I tripped over a diamond-studded hunk of meat.

In desperation I decided to secure myself to it,

hoping that a hungry bird would carry me to safety.

I waited nervously until a great vulture swooped down

and grabbed the meat. I was lifted high above the valley.

As the vulture landed with a jolt upon the mountain, men came screaming in from all directions, scaring the bird so much that it flew off, leaving its breakfast behind.
The men were alarmed to see me tied to the meat.

They would have killed me if I had not given them the diamonds embedded in it.
They then congratulated me on being the first man to come out of
the valley alive and offered to guide me home.

We journeyed together for many days and many nights, our route taking us over rough land and tumultuous seas.

We stopped only to sell our diamonds and the other goods we had bought during our long and profitable journey.

As we traveled, we saw several truly amazing sights. Strangest of all were the rhinoceroses grazing beneath the camphor trees. They were taller than camels, and their single horn was shaped in the likeness of a man.

When we finally reached Baghdad and I parted from my companions, I was a wealthy man once more.

I was able to share my good fortune with my family and friends. After some time, however, the sea called to me again.

That is the story of my second voyage.
Tomorrow, if Allah wills it, I shall tell you the tale of my third voyage—which, although you will find it hard to believe, was even more amazing."

SINBAD'S THIRD VOYAGE

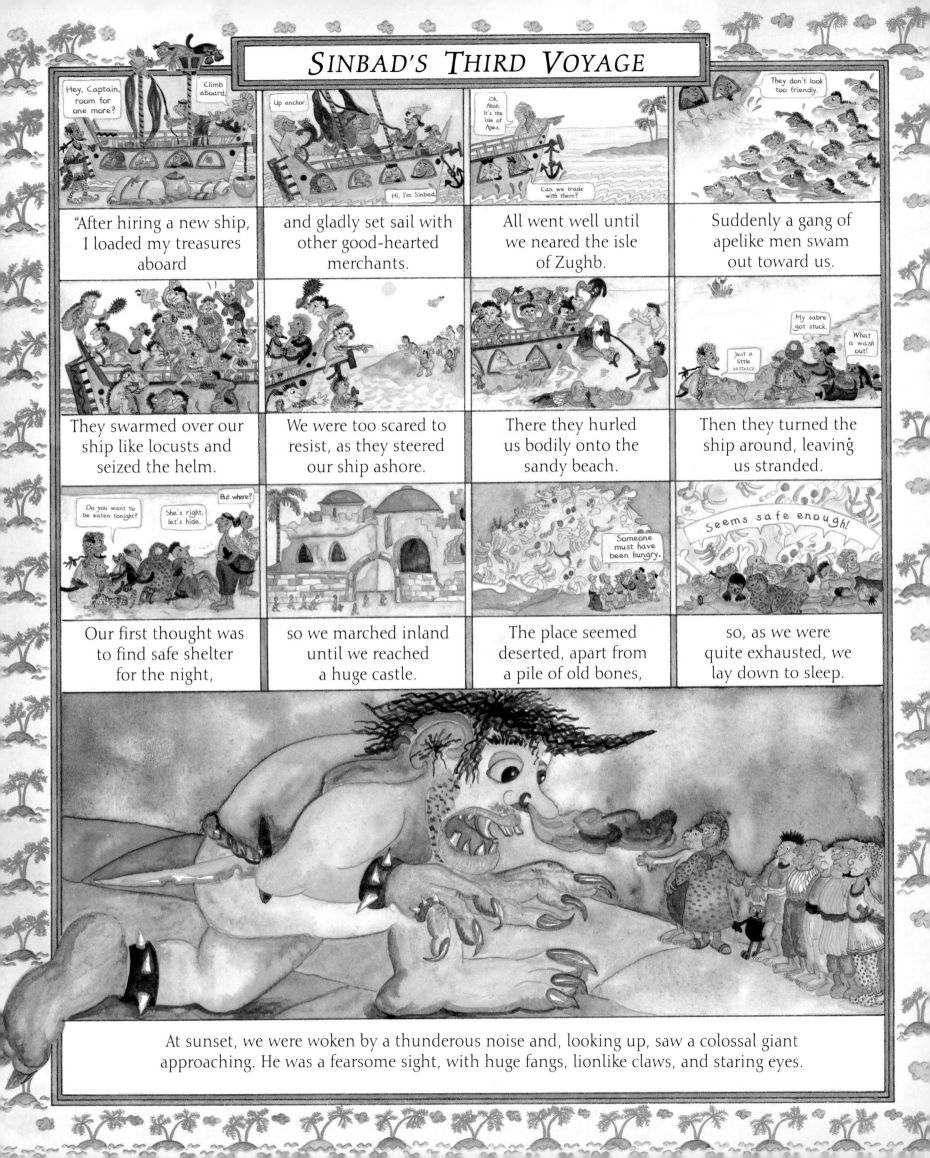

"After hiring a new ship, I loaded my treasures aboard

and gladly set sail with other good-hearted merchants.

All went well until we neared the isle of Zughb.

Suddenly a gang of apelike men swam out toward us.

They swarmed over our ship like locusts and seized the helm.

We were too scared to resist, as they steered our ship ashore.

There they hurled us bodily onto the sandy beach.

Then they turned the ship around, leaving us stranded.

Our first thought was to find safe shelter for the night,

so we marched inland until we reached a huge castle.

The place seemed deserted, apart from a pile of old bones,

so, as we were quite exhausted, we lay down to sleep.

At sunset, we were woken by a thunderous noise and, looking up, saw a colossal giant approaching. He was a fearsome sight, with huge fangs, lionlike claws, and staring eyes.

It was with great joy that I sailed away from that fearful island.

The captain was a kindly fellow. He fed and clothed me,

and, little by little, I regained my strength.

Imagine my delight on realizing that I was aboard the ship

that had sailed off and left me on the isle of the roc!

All my precious cargo was still on board.

As we sailed on from island to island,

I was able to trade, and I made a very pleasing profit,

so that when we reached Basra I was rich again.

I boarded a boat traveling upriver to Baghdad,

where my friends had gathered to give me a riotous welcome.

I willingly shared my wealth with rich and poor alike,

until my restless soul once more cried out for the sea.

That is the story of my third voyage.
Tomorrow, if Allah wills it, I shall tell you the tale of my fourth voyage—which,
although you will find it hard to believe, was even more amazing."

SINBAD'S FOURTH VOYAGE

"I took ship at Basra and sped from port to port across the foaming waves.

Then, one day, a great gale blew up, turning the waves to mountains and shattering our ship into many pieces. Most of my companions drowned. I and some others had the good fortune to catch hold of a floating beam.

We were washed onto a beach by the wind and waves.

Cold and wet from our ordeal, we started walking.

We eventually came to a lofty building surrounded by a forest of strange trees. As we drew closer, a number of wild-looking men emerged. Taking hold of us, they led us silently into the building.

Inside, their king was seated on his throne.

He called for food and ordered us to sit and eat.

My stomach revolted at the sight of food.

But my friends fell upon the feast, guzzling ravenously.

The more they ate, the more they seemed to want.

As they stuffed themselves, their stomachs grew

and their brains shrank. They became as beasts.

I knew then that the king of this island was a cannibal!

He was fattening up my friends making ready for a feast!

They were led away to be pastured in a field.

As I had eaten nothing and was only skin and bone,

the cannibals lost interest in me, and I was able to escape.

After walking for eight days, I met some peasants

who took me by boat to a neighboring isle.

The king of this island was a charming vegetarian.

It was a prosperous place, with many beautiful horses,

but not one person had ever heard of a saddle,

so I made a very beautiful one for the king.

Delighted with his gift, he gave me jewels galore,

and I became a happy and wealthy saddle maker.

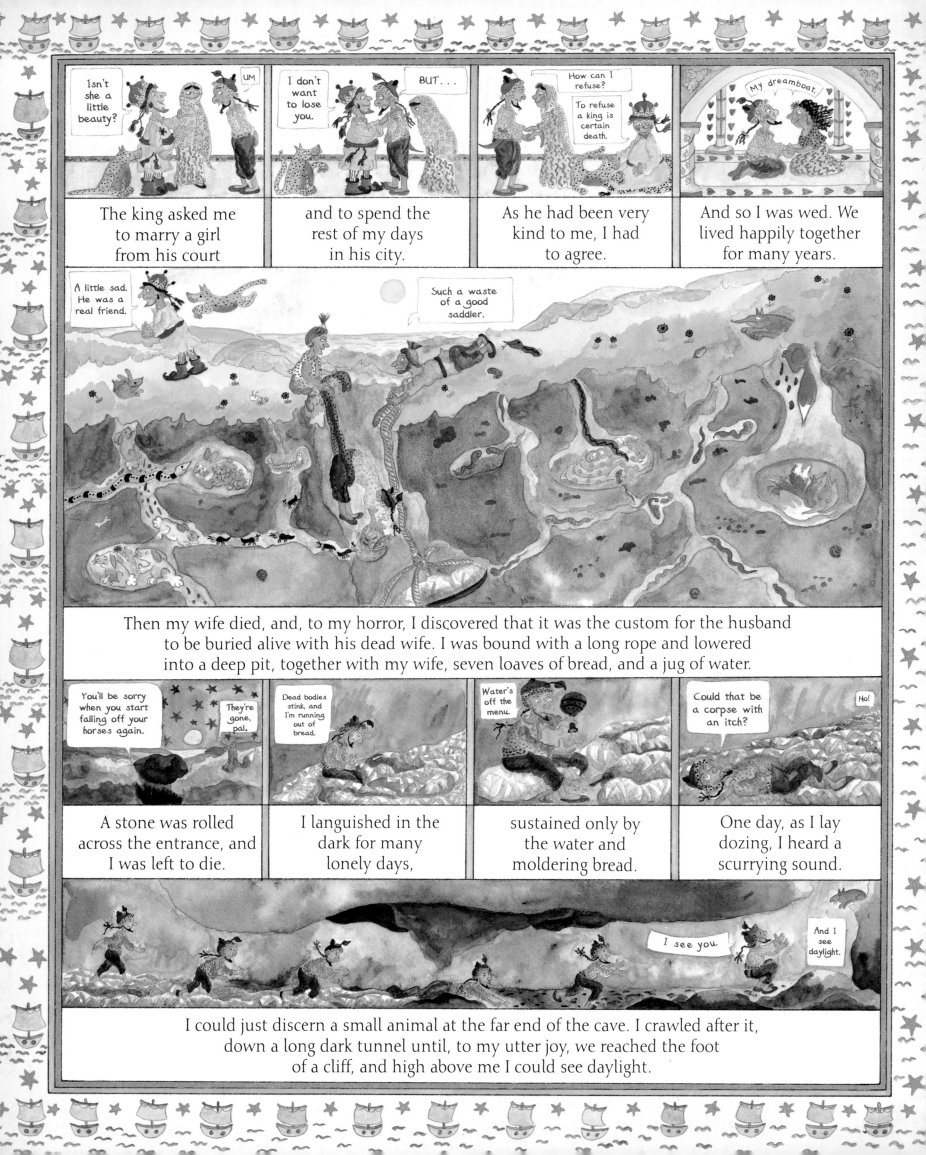

The king asked me to marry a girl from his court

and to spend the rest of my days in his city.

As he had been very kind to me, I had to agree.

And so I was wed. We lived happily together for many years.

Then my wife died, and, to my horror, I discovered that it was the custom for the husband to be buried alive with his dead wife. I was bound with a long rope and lowered into a deep pit, together with my wife, seven loaves of bread, and a jug of water.

A stone was rolled across the entrance, and I was left to die.

I languished in the dark for many lonely days,

sustained only by the water and moldering bread.

One day, as I lay dozing, I heard a scurrying sound.

I could just discern a small animal at the far end of the cave. I crawled after it, down a long dark tunnel until, to my utter joy, we reached the foot of a cliff, and high above me I could see daylight.

With an enormous effort, I struggled to the surface.

I rejoiced in the warmth of the sunshine.

I prayed to Allah that soon a ship would rescue me.

Meanwhile, I spent the time admiring the jewels hidden in my turban.

Eventually I saw a ship sailing close to shore. So, unwinding my turban, I tied it to a stick and ran up and down the beach, waving it frantically. Luckily, the crew saw me and sent a small boat ashore.

After many days' sailing the ship reached the port of Basra,

and although I was haunted by nightmares about the cavern,

I resumed my rich life—with the help of my jewels.

But the day came when I forgot my terrors and longed to go to sea again.

That is the story of my fourth voyage.
Tomorrow, if Allah wills it, I shall tell you the tale of my fifth voyage—which, although you will find it hard to believe, was even more amazing than my fourth."

SINBAD'S FIFTH VOYAGE

"I bought a fine ship with captain and crew, and, having loaded her with merchandise, set sail. I traded with people of many lands before we came to an island where we caught sight of a roc's egg.

My passengers went ashore to view this wonder but,

not content with just looking, they began throwing stones.

Alas, the egg was soon broken, revealing a chick inside,

which my foolish friends plucked, cooked and ATE!

Horrified at what they had done, I got them aboard and weighed anchor as quickly as possible. Unfortunately, not quickly enough, for soon the world around us grew dark, as the gigantic rocs arrived to take their revenge.

The huge birds aimed such large boulders at us that great chasms opened in the sea. Finally, they scored a direct hit upon my ship, crushing many of my crew and hurling others into the sea to be swallowed by the waves.

The furious monkeys retaliated by hurling coconuts at us. These we gathered until our sacks bulged.

We then returned to the city and sold the coconuts for an excellent profit. I did this several times.

Soon I could afford my passage back to Basra.

On the way, I was able to sell more coconuts,

and when we reached the Sea of Pearls

I hired several skilled divers to work for me.

In a short time I had a hoard of priceless pearls,

so, once more, I was returning a rich man.

On reaching home I was greeted by my friends.

I shared my wealth with them and the poor.

I lived a delightful life of ease until I made the mistake of entertaining a group of adventurers, who reminded me of the pleasures and excitement of traveling the high seas. And so I felt the urge, eventually, to leave home once again.

That is the story of my fifth voyage. Tomorrow, if Allah wills it, I shall tell you the story of my sixth voyage—which, although you will find it hard to believe, was even more amazing."

SINBAD'S SIXTH VOYAGE

"Having set sail from Basra with a rich cargo, we voyaged leisurely for a time, remembering all the strange and wonderful things we had seen on other voyages.

One day, in midocean, the captain burst into a loud lament, as the ship had been driven into unknown and dangerous waters. Just as we were turning around . . .

a great wind arose, dashing our ship upon the rocks. Many of my companions were drowned, but others, like myself, clung to the rocks and dragged themselves ashore.

The sands were littered with other wrecks and their valuable cargo, and the whole place was lit up by a jewel-encrusted river that flowed into a dark cavern.

There seemed no way to escape, and the days dragged by as we waited for our food to run out and then for death. One by one I buried my companions, until I alone was left.

I began to dig myself a grave in which to lie as death approached. But as I dug, I began to think that every river must have a beginning and an end, so I made myself a raft from aloe wood.

Having loaded it with sacks of gems and ambergris, I launched myself upon the river. The current tossed me from side to side, carrying me deep into the cavern's darkness.

As the passage narrowed, I was forced onto my belly. Faster and faster I was swept along until, overcome by fear, I fell into a deathlike sleep.

I awoke to find myself close to a bank and surrounded by Indians and Abyssinians.
They brought me food, and, with the help of one who could speak Arabic, I told my story.

They then formed a long procession and carried me and my cargo to their king,
Serendib, so that he, too, could marvel at my adventure and lucky escape.

The king greeted me warmly and listened in astonishment to my tale. He was delighted
when I presented him with some of the finest jewels I had collected on the beach.

He invited me to be his guest, and we spent many happy hours
discussing the merits of each other's countries and methods of government.

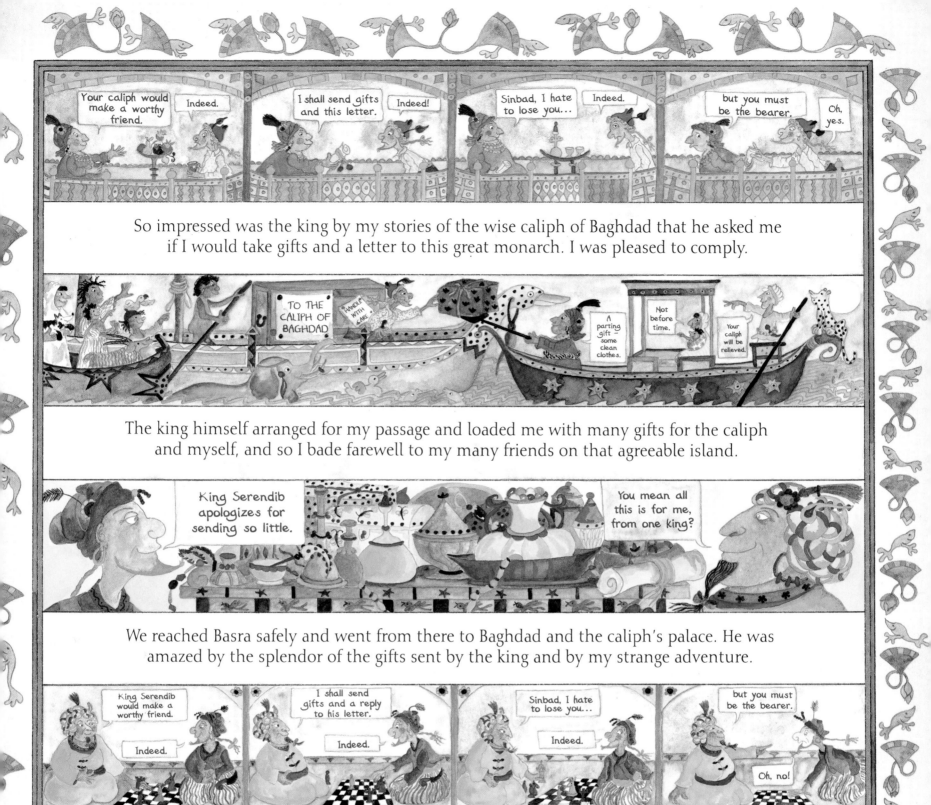

So impressed was the king by my stories of the wise caliph of Baghdad that he asked me if I would take gifts and a letter to this great monarch. I was pleased to comply.

The king himself arranged for my passage and loaded me with many gifts for the caliph and myself, and so I bade farewell to my many friends on that agreeable island.

We reached Basra safely and went from there to Baghdad and the caliph's palace. He was amazed by the splendor of the gifts sent by the king and by my strange adventure.

After this, I firmly resolved to stay at home. But then one day, while I was visiting the caliph, he said that the time had come for me to carry his presents to King Serendib.

That is the story of my sixth voyage.
Tomorrow, if Allah wills it, I shall tell you the story of my seventh voyage—which, although you will find it hard to believe, was even more amazing."

SINBAD'S SEVENTH VOYAGE

This is my last voyage, or my name's not Sinbad.

Sailing without mishap is rather boring.

Oh dear, there's Serendib and not one adventure to tell of.

Oh, good, the return of Sinbad. Now I'll hear some fishy tales!

"Most unwillingly, I set sail for the island of Serendib with the caliph's letter and a cargo of gifts. The journey took two long months, but we finally arrived without mishap.

You're most welcome, Sinbad. I can't wait to hear your latest adventure.

You must stay a year or two so you can tell us every detail!

Well, I suppose even the great Sinbad has to retire some time.

The king was overjoyed to see me and to be honored so by the caliph. He wanted me to stay with him, but I was anxious to return home to Baghdad so only stayed long enough to reload.

Maybe I'm too old for adventures.

Never mind the ship, save the cargo.

We journeyed home peacefully for many days. Then a sudden tempest hit the ship, drenching our cargo with rain. As we struggled to cover it, a terrible roar rose from the sea.

There goes my cargo.

Looking around, we saw a great sea monster rushing toward us. It seized our ship in its vast jaws, and as I dived off the side it swallowed it down in one gulp.

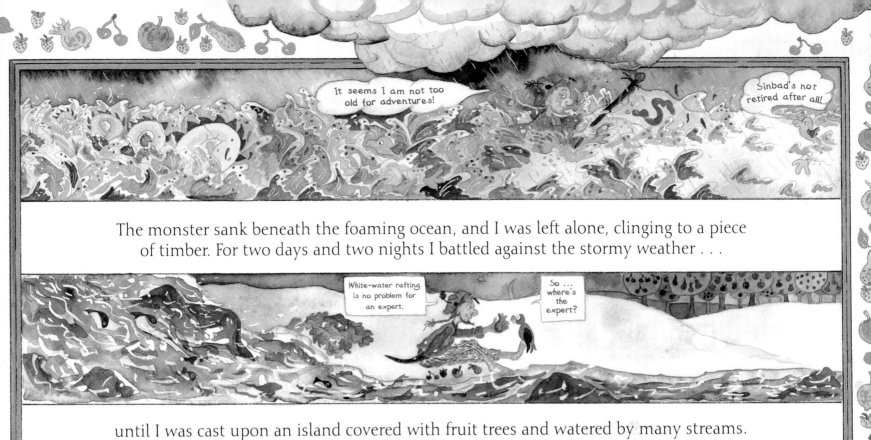

The monster sank beneath the foaming ocean, and I was left alone, clinging to a piece
of timber. For two days and two nights I battled against the stormy weather . . .

until I was cast upon an island covered with fruit trees and watered by many streams.
I wandered around until I came to a fast-flowing river which I resolved to travel down by raft.

I made a sturdy raft from some exotic wood and pushed off downriver. I sped along on the
current at great speed; faster and faster I sped until I realized I must be heading for a precipice.

Resigning myself to death, I closed my eyes. Then, as the raft reached the very edge, I felt it halt.
Opening my eyes, I found I had been saved by a net thrown by some men on the bank.

The men hauled me over to the muddy bank.

I lay there exhausted until an old man kindly helped me up

and took me to the city baths, where I was washed.

Afterward, he took me to his house and cared for me.

He even said he would help me sell my wares,

which puzzled me, as I was unaware of having any.

At the market I discovered that he meant my raft.

It was made of sandalwood and sold for a fortune.

I stayed happily with the old man for some time.

When he asked me to marry his beautiful daughter,

I was unable to refuse such a genial host.

Luckily we grew to love each other dearly.

When the old man died, I inherited his wealth

and continued to live happily with his daughter.

Then I found that once a year the local men grew wings

and for a whole day flew high above the city.

Eager to join them, I persuaded a friend to let me ride on his back. All went well until we flew so close to Heaven that I heard the angels sing. 'Praise be to Allah,' I cried, and at once we plummeted back to earth.

Sinbad the Sailor and Sinbad the Porter vowed to remain friends.

Thereafter, they spent many happy hours together, playing with their model ships and discussing the wonders and terrors of Sinbad the Sailor's seven amazing voyages.